SHADO

A SENS
STUD
SIMPLEST, SAFEST, AND MOST STUPENDOUS FORM OF ENTERTAINMENT THAT MAN HAS EVER KNOWN. WITHOUT A SHADOW OF A DOUBT THE MOST SURPRISING SHOW ON EARTH.

Other books by GYLES BRANDRETH

1000 JOKES: THE GREATEST JOKE BOOK EVER
1000 FACTS: THE GRATEST FACT BOOK EVER
1000 RIDDLES: THE GREATEST BOOK OF RIDDLES
1000 QUESTIONS: THE GREATEST QUIZ BOOK
CRAZY DAYS
THE BIG BOOK OF MAGIC
THE BIG BOOK OF PRACTICAL JOKES
THE BIG BOOK OF SECRETS
THE CRAZY ENCYCLOPAEDIA
THE CRAZY WORD BOOK
THE DAFT DICTIONARY
THE BIG BOOK OF OPTICAL ILLUSIONS
JOKES! JOKES! JOKES!
PROJECT: THE HUMAN BODY
PROJECT: NUMBER FUN

Published by CAROUSEL BOOKS

SHADOW SHOWS
A CAROUSEL BOOK 0 552 54192 3

First published in Great Britain by Carousel Books

PRINTING HISTORY
Carousel edition published 1981

Carousel Books are published by
Transworld Publishers Ltd.,
Century House, 61–63 Uxbridge Road,
Ealing, London W5 5SA.

Printed and bound in Great Britain by
Cox & Wyman Ltd., Reading

GYLES BRANDRETH
Illustrated by David Farris

CAROUSEL BOOKS
A DIVISION OF TRANSWORLD PUBLISHERS LTD.

For in and out, above, about, below,
Tis nothing but a Magic SHADOW SHOW
Play'd in a box whose candle is the Sun,
Round which we phantom figures run.

The Rubaiyat of Omar Khayyam

What is always with you, follows you closely everywhere, is behind you even when you can't see it, yet you can't touch it or feel it either?

Yes, of course – your shadow!!

I am sure that at some time or another you have looked at your own shadow and noticed how it changes in shape and size according to where you are standing and the position of the sun in the sky – sometimes it looks as if you are a very tall giant, and at other times it looks like a short fat dwarf – but I wonder if you have ever realised what tremendous fun shadows can be, or what amazing and amusing things you can do with them? If not, then this book can open up a whole new world for you and show you how easy it is to create your own sensational shadow shows. You will not only be able to amaze your friends, but with them to help you, you can put on a real show to entertain your parents and the rest of the family too. Don't worry about your pets either because even they can help you in your exciting **SHADOW SHOWS**.

Read on . . .

WHAT YOU WILL NEED . . .

Mounting your own Shadow Show can be very simple indeed. All you really require is a lamp of some kind (a flexible desk lamp is best, but even a strong torch will do), and a wall or screen on which to cast your shadows.

The best time to try making shadows is when it is dark. Find a light coloured wall, or fix a piece of light coloured paper to the wall (do ask before you stick pins in as they could damage the wall). Then put a torch or lamp on a table and shine it at the wall.

Now, all you need is this book, a pair of hands, and after a little practice you'll be able to create your very own shadows.

HAND SHADOWS

Many many thousands of years ago, long before you or I were born, even before your grandparents or great-aunt Doris were born, two cavemen called Uglin and Oglo sat around a huge roaring fire in their cave one very cold winters evening, roasting a brontosaurus leg for their supper.

As the meat began to sizzle, Uglin reached out his hand to see if their supper was ready. Suddenly the shadow of a huge hungry wolf appeared on the wall of the cave, obviously the delicious smell of roast dinosaur had attracted it to the cave. Oglo grabbed hold of Uglin in fear and the shadow disappeared.

After a while, all seemed quiet and as the meat appeared to be burning, Uglin reached out once more. Again the giant wolf's shadow appeared on the wall. Each time Uglin put out his hand it appeared and when he took it away, the wolf vanished. It was then the two cavemen realised that the shadow cast upon the wall was really that of Uglin's hand, and the firelight had made it appear so large.

Uglin and Oglo began to experiment and found that by changing the position of their hands, they could make all sorts of animal shadows appear on the wall. They didn't worry that their supper was ruined, this was far more fun – they had invented the very first **Hand Shadow Show**!

Hand shadows are very easy to produce and soon you will be able to invent your own incredible and original shadows. To begin with it is best to follow the examples on the next few pages. If you put your hands carefully into the positions shown in the drawings (you'll find them very handy!) you'll see similar shadows appearing on your walls. Try it and see!

Do remember . . .

1. When making shadows, keep the light close enough so that your shadows are crisp and clear, not blurred.

2. Roll up your sleeves and remove your watch, so that your arms are bare.

3. Always look at the shadows on the wall, not at your hands – once the shadow is how you want it to be **then** look at your hands to see what position your fingers are in. You'll find this becomes easier in time.

4. Don't lose hope if your first attempts are unsuccessful, and don't strain your fingers – if they get tired, rest them for a while. You'll be surprised at how suddenly your shadows begin to take shape.

You are now ready to begin . . .

Here is a **pigeon**, or maybe a **sparrow** –

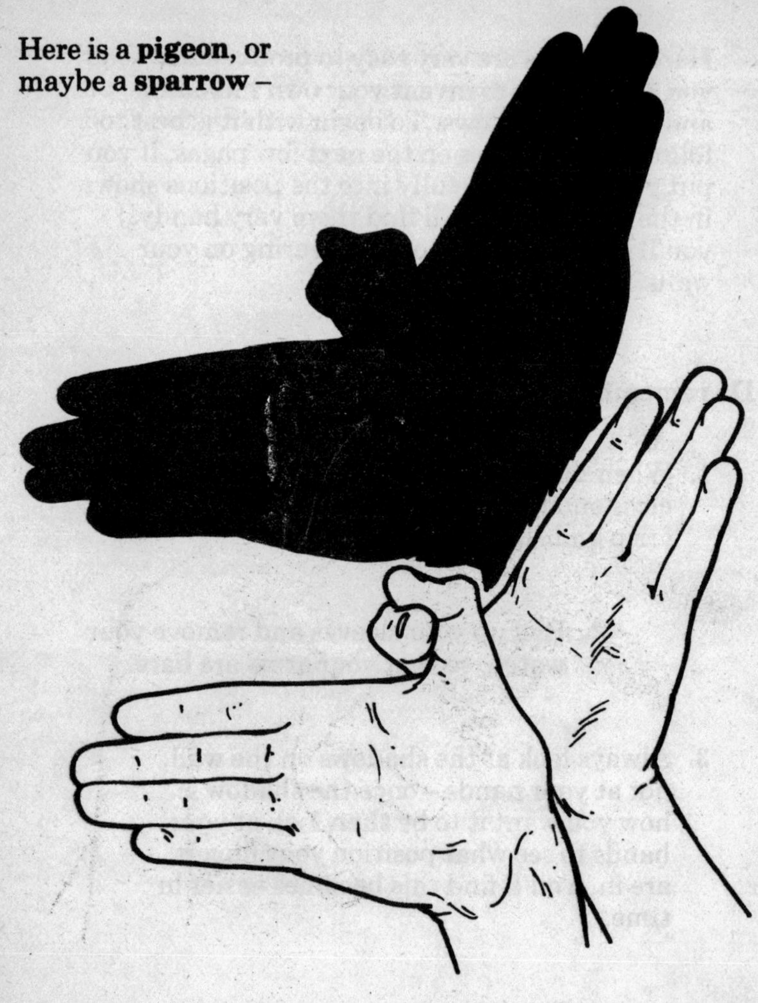

Now try moving your hands backwards and forwards and you'll find the bird actually looks as if it is flying. Perhaps, if you position yourself carefully, you will be able to convince your mother that there is a phantom bat or wild bird on the loose in your bedroom!

One of the best-loved hand shadows, and always a favourite at shadow shows, is the **rabbit**. If you intend to give a Shadow Show then this is a good one to start with.

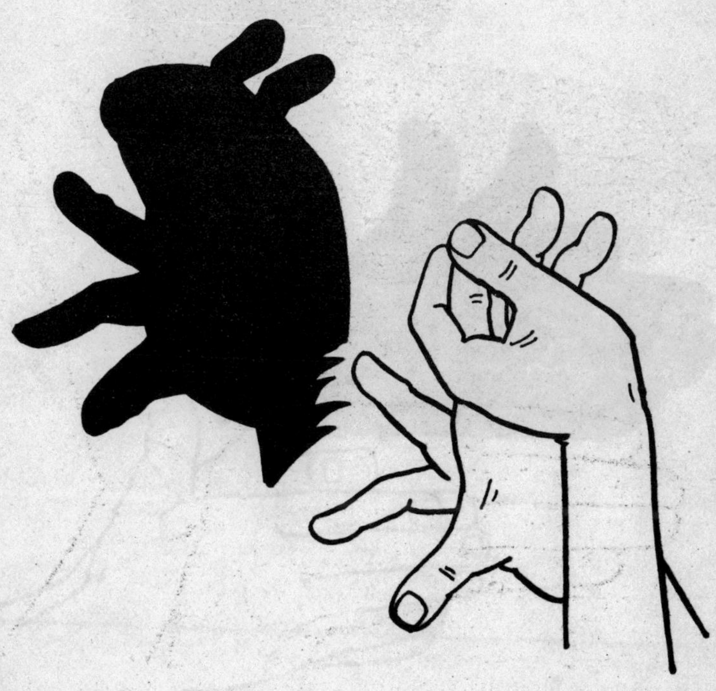

By the way, where do rabbits go when they get married?

On a "bunnymoon"!!

If you happen to have some pet lovers at your Shadow Show then it's a good idea to give them something they'll instantly recognise. You can tell them that it's the best **dog** in the world because it doesn't need taking for a walk, and never gets fleas!

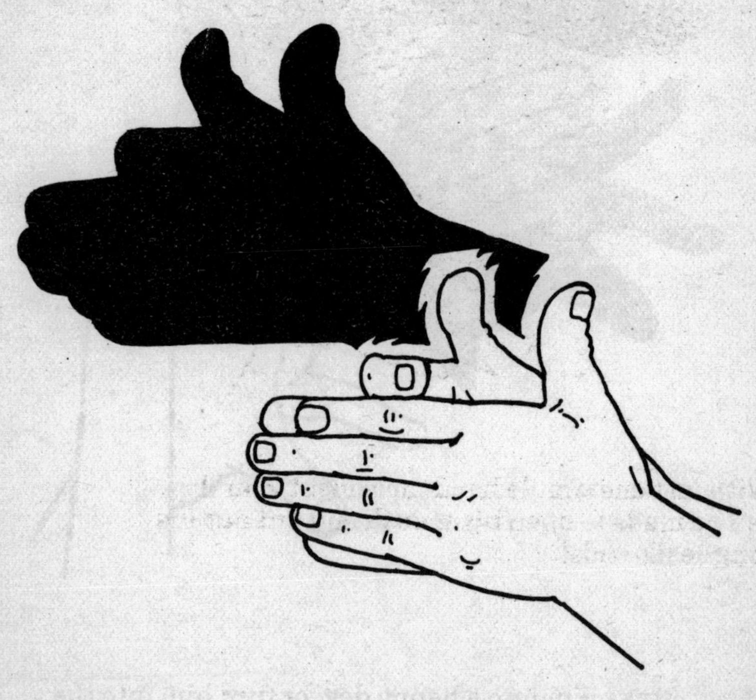

My dog thinks he's a chicken. I'd take him to a vet, only I need the eggs!

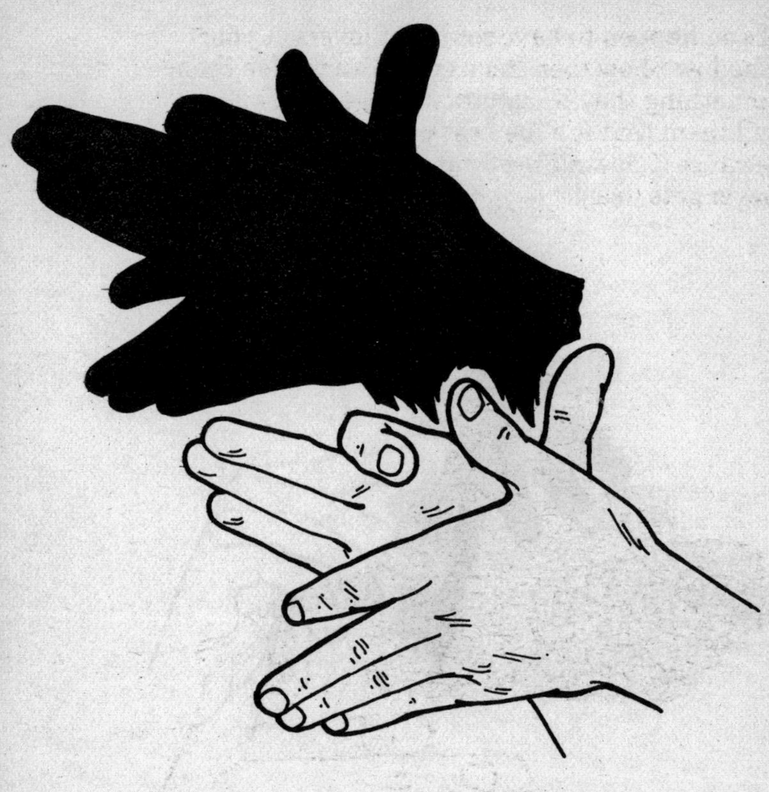

With just one simple hand movement your dog can be made to **open his mouth** and **put out his tongue** like this!

Make him into a happy dog, or turn him into the Hound of the Baskervilles and have everyone riveted to their seats. Better still, turn him into a watch-dog and tell them the time!

With a bit more practice you will soon be able to create this wordy-birdy – yes, a **parrot**. By putting your hands closer to the light you can make it as big as a lion! When a parrot this size says: **"Who's a pretty boy?"**, you'd better listen!

Of course, you don't have to stick to making shadows of animals, you can just as easily make shadows of **human faces** with your hands. Try making a shadow of one of your family, or perhaps one of your favourite television personalities, even a cartoon character. Maybe even yourself – you may not have your name up in lights, but you can have your face on a wall!

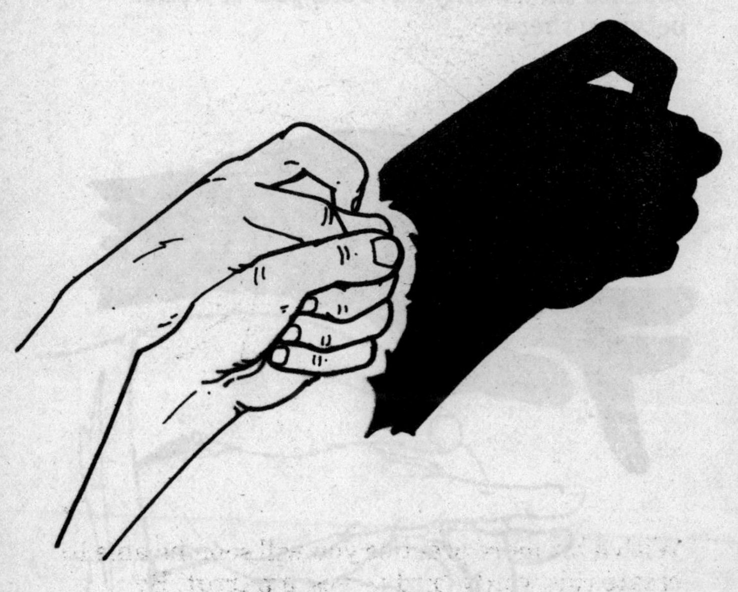

What did one wall say to the other wall?

"I'll meet you at the corner."

Why do elephants have big ears?

Because Noddy wouldn't pay them the ransom money!

Elephants are always popular and you can make one as big, or as small, as you like. Why not get a friend to help you and then you can have two elephants, but don't let them go swimming because they'll only have one pair of trunks between them!

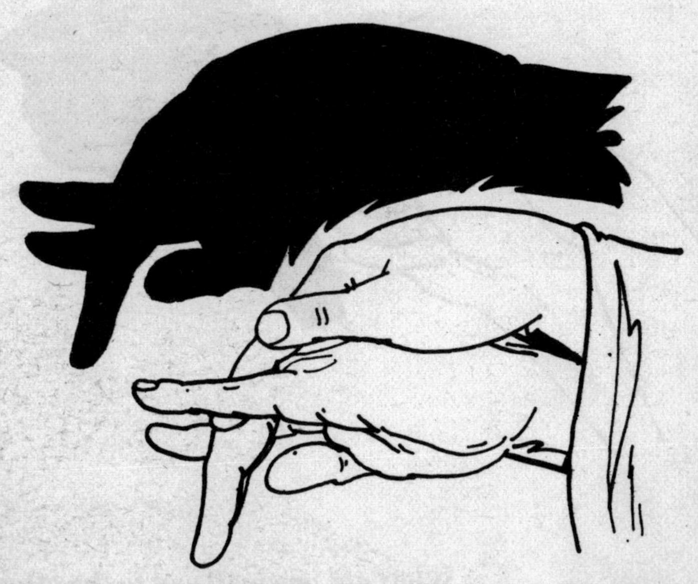

What do you get if you cross an elephant with a mouse?

Great big holes in your skirting-board!

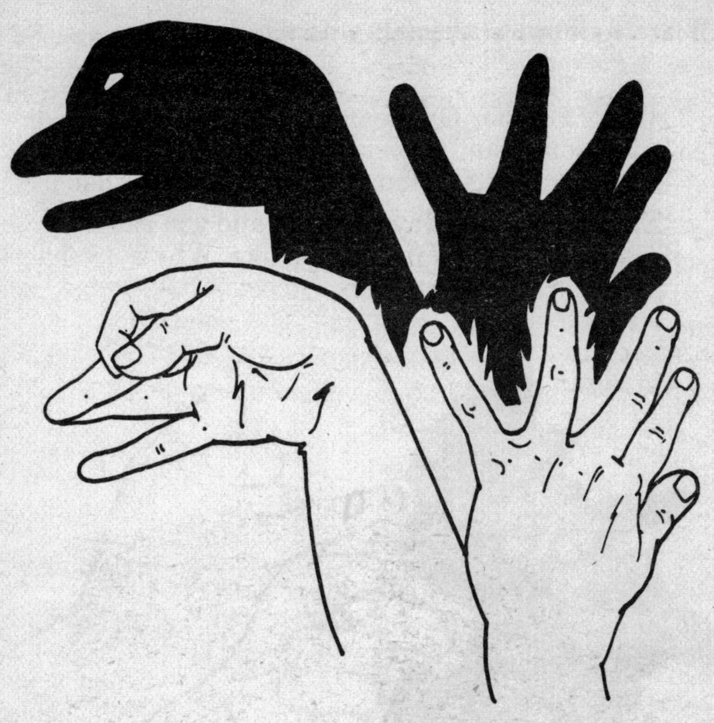

Why did the duck say: "QUICK! QUICK!"?

Because it was in a hurry.

You don't have to be quackers to put **Dilys Duck** into action – and if your mother has always wanted ducks flying up the wall, this could be the answer!

Create your own characters with hand shadows –

Here is **Farmer Gyles**, try giving him a voice and before long you'll have your own unique character. Practise moving your fingers so that you can make his mouth open and close, just as if he was really talking.

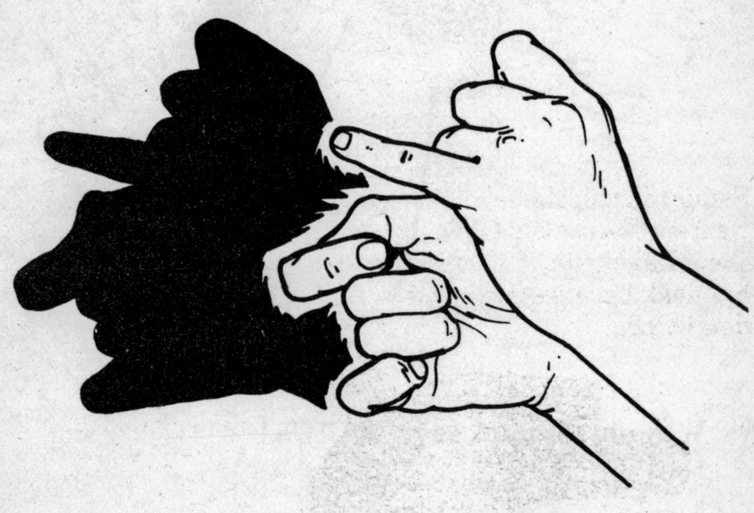

Farmer Gyles looks very cross, doesn't he. That's because someone just trod on his corn!

With a few friends to help you, you can create some of the talking animals at the same time and perhaps make up a little story about life on the farm.

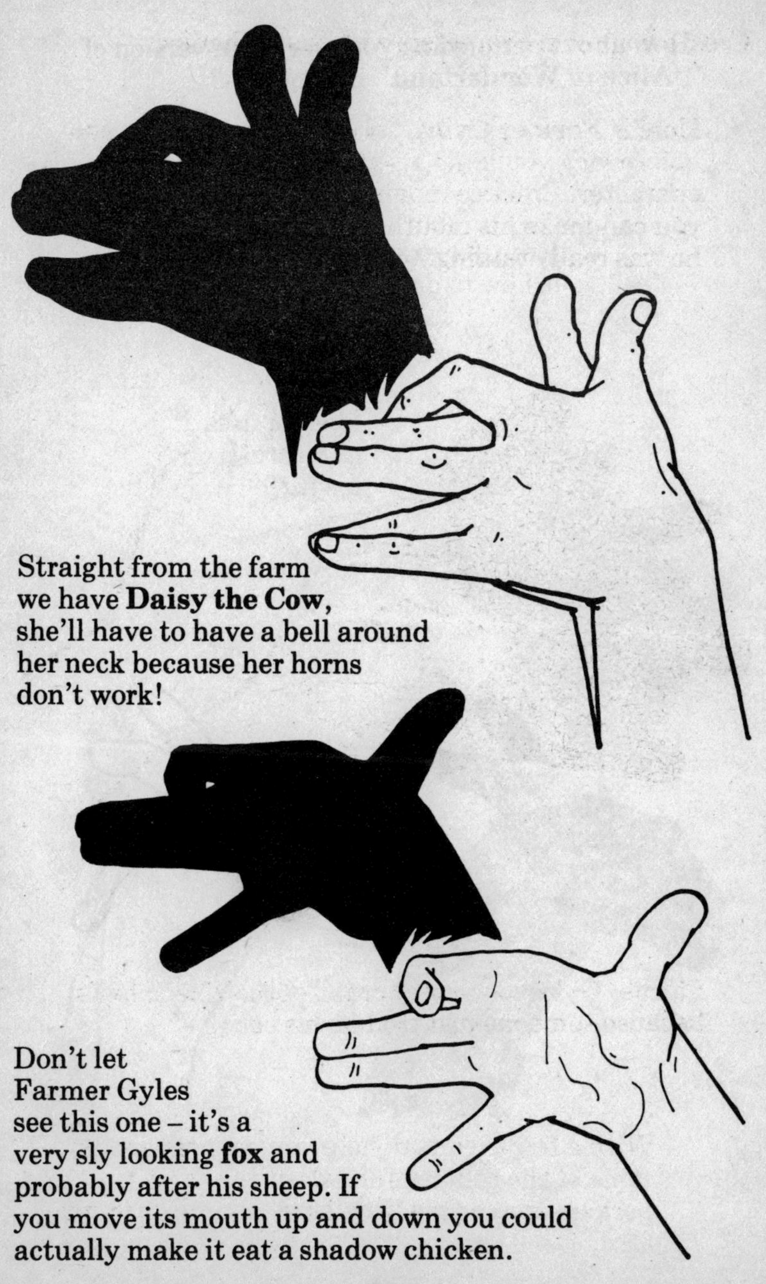

Straight from the farm
we have **Daisy the Cow**,
she'll have to have a bell around
her neck because her horns
don't work!

Don't let
Farmer Gyles
see this one – it's a
very sly looking **fox** and
probably after his sheep. If
you move its mouth up and down you could
actually make it eat a shadow chicken.

How about performing your very own version of **"Alice in Wonderland"** in shadows?

Here, for example,
is how to do the **March Hare**.

I bet he uses a
hare-brush on
his fur!

If you're striving for purr-fection then the following shadow is for you. It is, of course, a **cat** – perhaps the **Cheshire Cat** from Wonderland.

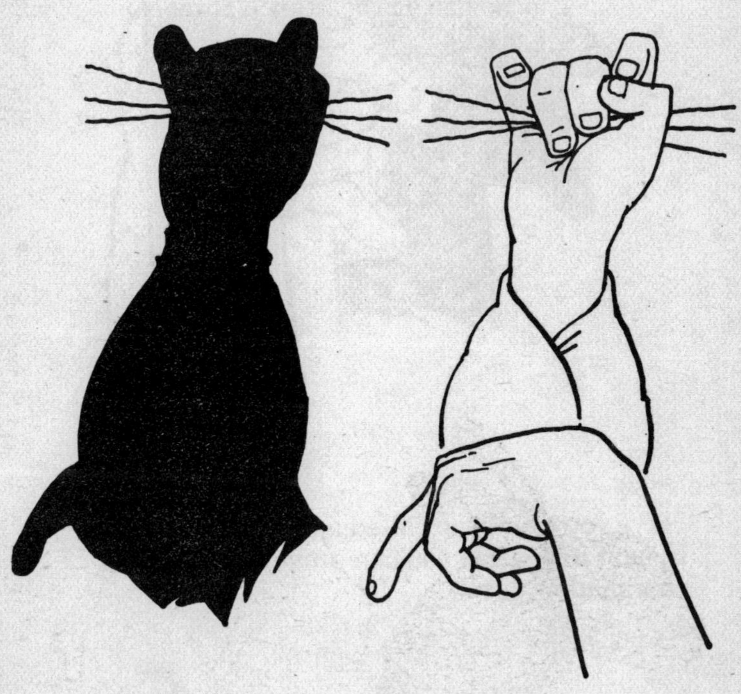

This one is a little more difficult as you will need a few props – a **handkerchief** or scarf around your arm, and three carefully positioned **drinking-straws** for the whiskers.

Have you ever been called a "little devil"? Well in next to no time you can prove it's true with this shadow **devil**.

And if mum or dad happens to have a red light-bulb that you could use in your lamp, then you can make him look even more realistic.

Here's **Humphrey the Camel.**

If a friend doesn't mind lending a hand you can give him as many humps as you like. Camels are very interesting creatures. I bet you didn't know that they drink litres of water before starting a journey so that they can survive in the desert for a long time without needing a drink, and there are no camel hairs in camel-hair paint brushes!

This dog will dash into a corner every time he hears the doorbell ring – that's because he's a **boxer**!

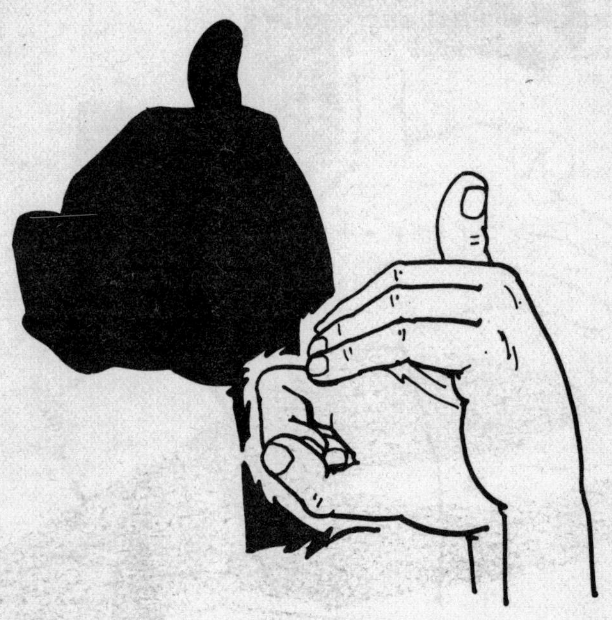

Be patriotic and include a traditional **British Bulldog** in your show too, this shadow can be made into either of these two dogs.

If you want to do a Christmas Shadow Show, how about trying Peter Pan – then this shadow could be used for the **crocodile**.

Do you know what a crocodile's favourite game is?

Snap!

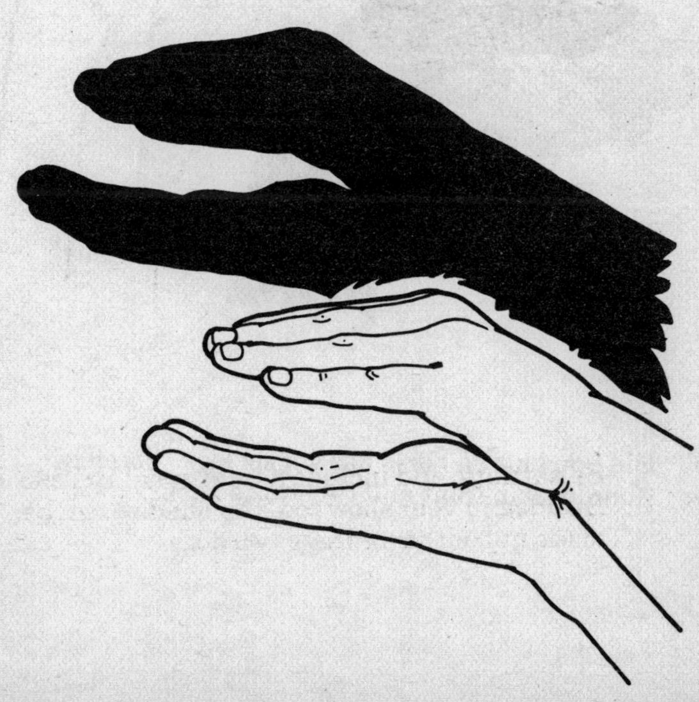

With just one hand you can quickly create this simple, but very impressive **horse**.

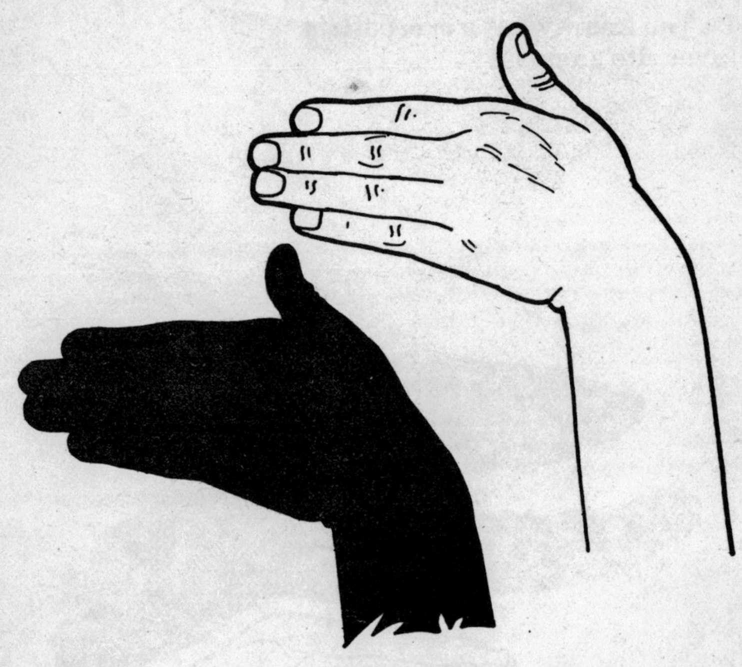

Did you know a horse has got six legs? Forelegs (four legs) in front and two at the back.

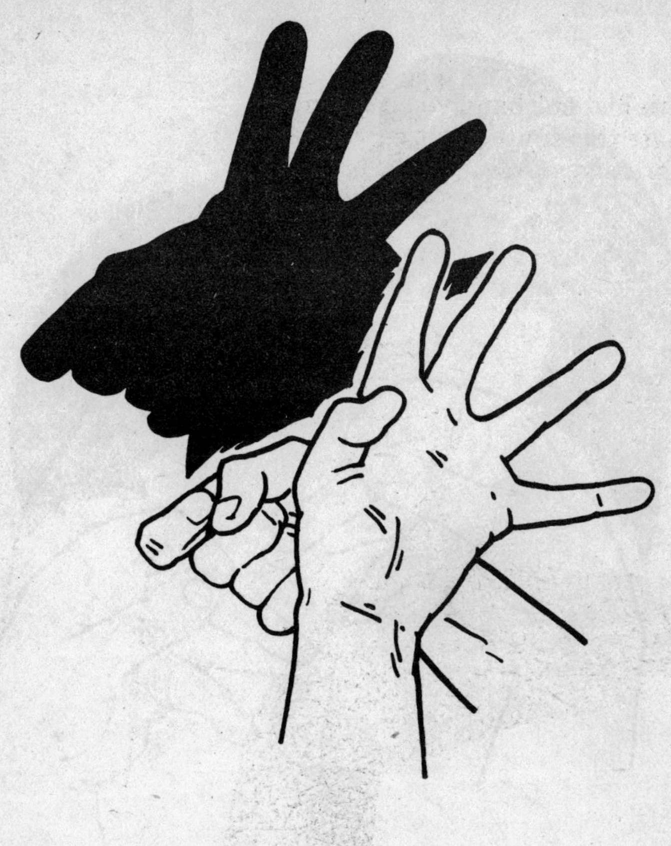

This is **Tom O'Hawk the Indian**, he's only little so his laugh is more of a mini-ha-ha.

Why not create a few cowboys and soon you can produce your own western!

Finally . . . **Gertie Goose** and **Gordon Gander** could soon become a popular double act like Laurel and Hardy.

Try writing them some comic dialogue to use in their act, like this:

GERTIE: What's worse than an elephant with a blocked nose?

GORDON: I don't know, what?

GERTIE: A tortoise with claustrophobia.

GORDON: OK, if you're so clever – why did the old lady put her hands over her ears when she passed the hen house?

GERTIE: Because she didn't want to hear their foul language?

It is important to learn the hand positions for all these characters off by heart so that you can produce your shadows as quickly as possible. Then you will be ready to perform your first Shadow Show.

Only perform the shadows that you can do really well. If you copy one of the examples and find it turns out looking different but still interesting – like a pig or a rhinoceros – don't worry, include it in your act! Everybody's hands are different and will produce different shadows, that is part of the fun!

Plan your show carefully, and don't make it too long otherwise it does tend to become boring. Arrange your act carefully, start with something like the rabbit that is instantly recognisable. Do the simple shadows first and save the most complicated, and the one you can do best, until last.

When performing, do position yourself carefully – make sure the audience have a clear view of the surface you are casting your shadows on, and position yourself to the side, between your lamp and your screen. You will probably find it easier if you sit down to do your shadows.

Good luck with the Show!

FIGURE SHADOWS

Hand shadows can be fun to perform, but you don't have to limit yourself to using just your hands. You can use your **whole body** to create life-like and sometimes very comical characters.

Here is an example:

To produce some very impressive figure shadows you need plenty of imagination and as many old clothes, hats, and pieces of cardboard as you can find.

Remember, the colour and texture of your costumes is not important because all you require for a shadow is the **SHAPE**. So if you want to have shadows of witches you don't have to dress yourself in black, what you need is a **pointed cardboard hat** and a **sheet** or **old curtain** to use as a cloak.

There is no limit to the number of shadow figures that you can create. **Wigs** can be made out of wool or string, the colour is not important. Don't forget to use props to help define your character – for example a **saucepan** and a **spoon** if you are going to be a chef, and perhaps a big **pepper-pot**!

If you are going to put on a **Figure Shadow Show** then you will need more than just a blank wall. If you are really going to impress your audience you will need a large white sheet. Try not to get any creases in it, otherwise it won't make a very good screen.

Pin the sheet to the ceiling of the room in which you intend to perform your shadow plays, about two-thirds of the way along the room. Have the door in the smaller section, as this is going to be your stage and the door will be your stage entrance. Outside the door will be your "wings". This is where everyone will wait before coming on stage and where they can put their costumes on.

Make sure also that the sheet stays still as it will spoil your shadows if it moves about. Put something heavy at each end to weight it down.

Now position your light behind the screen, so that there is plenty of room for you to perform between the lamp and the screen. Your audience will be sitting on the other side and so all they will see will be your shadows, for them it will be like sitting in a cinema!

Once your audience are seated and you are ready to begin, turn all the lights out just for a couple of minutes, this will make your lamp seem much brighter to the audience when you turn it on – now you are ready to begin your show.

Plan your show very carefully and make sure that you have rehearsed it well with your friends. One useful point to remember is not to have too many shadows on the screen at any one time as it confuses the audience. Try and only have *two* characters on stage at the same time.

Try and make up your own plays, or enact a well-known fairy story using very **recognisable characters**, like the Mad Hatter or a pirate. Don't attempt something with too many characters like Ali Baba and his Forty Thieves. However a simple pantomime is a good idea at Christmas. Later in this book you will find a couple of Shadow Plays to perform.

Here are a few ideas for character shadows . . .

Try being **Cinderella's Ugly Sister** – you can give them outrageous hair-styles, and make one of them very, very fat by putting a cushion or a pillow inside the costume. See what sort of shadow you can get then!

Dick Whittington and his Cat

Have your very own **Mad Hatter's tea party**! Create all Lewis Carroll's loveable characters from the Dormouse to Alice herself. Make all your props out of carboard from tea-pot to top-hat – soon everyone will be raising their hats to you!

Try making a **clown shadow** – all you need is a pointed hat and a ping-pong ball for a nose – make sure your shadow is in profile though.

Perhaps if you are unsure about what to perform and cannot find a suitable play to act, then choose one of your **favourite stories** or **poems**. Have one person as a narrator, that is the person who reads the story aloud, and then the rest of you mime the story in figure shadows as it is read out.

Remember that your costumes do not have to be elaborate or expensive, a **cardboard crown** and a **blanket** will make a very impressive shadow of a king, and don't forget to have lots of props such as **walking sticks**, **tomahawks**, **guns**, and so on. The way you **stand** is important too – upright if you are meant to be young, or bent over if you are meant to be very old.

If you are feeling very adventurous then try experimenting with **masks** to create very stunning effects. For example, by giving yourself a **long beak** you can make a giant bird. Or give yourself large **angel** or **fairy wings**.

Very exciting effects can be achieved if, as part of a fairy costume, you make a wire frame as an outline for the wings and cover them (get your mother to help you if you cannot sew) with a very thin material – such as a nylon or chiffon scarf.

The light will shine through, giving you a very interesting shadow.

Why not try your own **horror show** and scare your audience out of their wits!

The fact that they are seated in the dark will help. A monster can easily be created by putting a **piece of wood inside your jacket** to make your shoulders appear very big and stiff, like Frankenstein – and perhaps even a papier mache head could be made too with a bolt through the neck!

A **Ghost** can be made very simply by putting a sheet over your head, and the shape can be made very frightening by moving nearer to your lamp as this will make the shadow much larger and give the appearance that it is growing.

This could be used very effectively if you do a version of Aladdin and his Genie, for the genie can be made to grow –

What do monsters have every night at 10.30?

A coffin break!

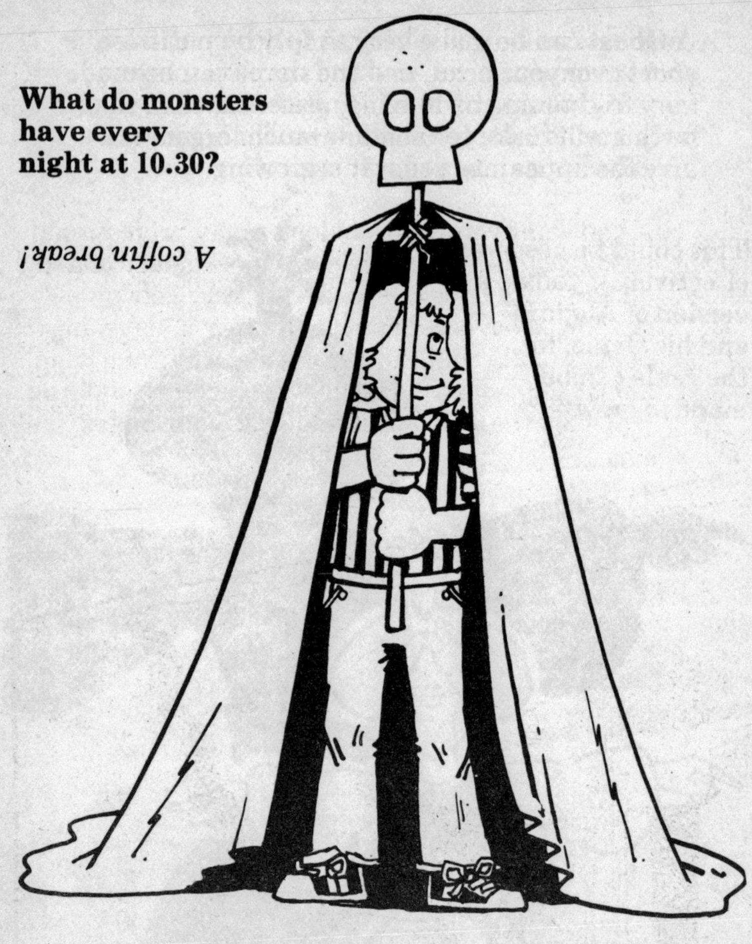

If you want a **spook shadow**, then a very frightening ghost can be made from a couple of wooden rods, an old sheet and a cardboard mask cut out in the shape of a skull.

As the stick is raised and lowered the ghost shadow will appear to float and will also be able to grow enormously tall.

Once you've figured out what to do you can let your imagination run riot and develop some fantastic figure shadows. By standing close to or far from the lamp your shadows can be made as large or as small as you want.

If you want your plays to look really professional then try adding some scenery too – a **cardboard cut-out of a tree** will produce a very good shadow, even a **beanstalk shadow** if you want to perform Jack and the Beanstalk. Anything from a boat to a house. Once you've started you'll find you have the world of shadows at your finger tips!

SHADOW PUPPETS

For a shadow puppet show you need a new and different kind of screen. This is because the people operating the puppets must be kept hidden, and also it is important that your audience does not see how the puppet works as this would spoil everything.

The best way to present a Shadow Puppet Show is to have a small screen made, like a very large picture frame. It needs to be about one metre long by sixty centimetres wide, depending of course upon the size of your table and your puppets. If you aren't a handy carpenter yourself, ask someone who is to help you make the frame.

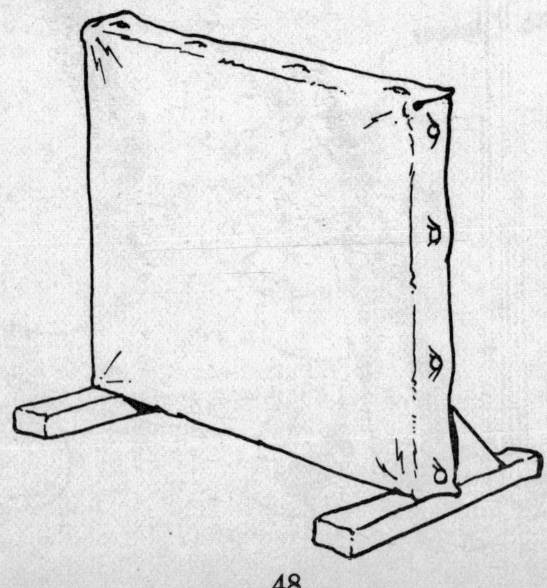

The frame can stand on a table top, you can sit one side of it and your audience the other. If you are feeling really ingenious you can cut out some pieces of cardboard or material as decoration and, with some paint, turn your screen into a real puppet theatre!

Place a torch or small lamp quite close to the screen.

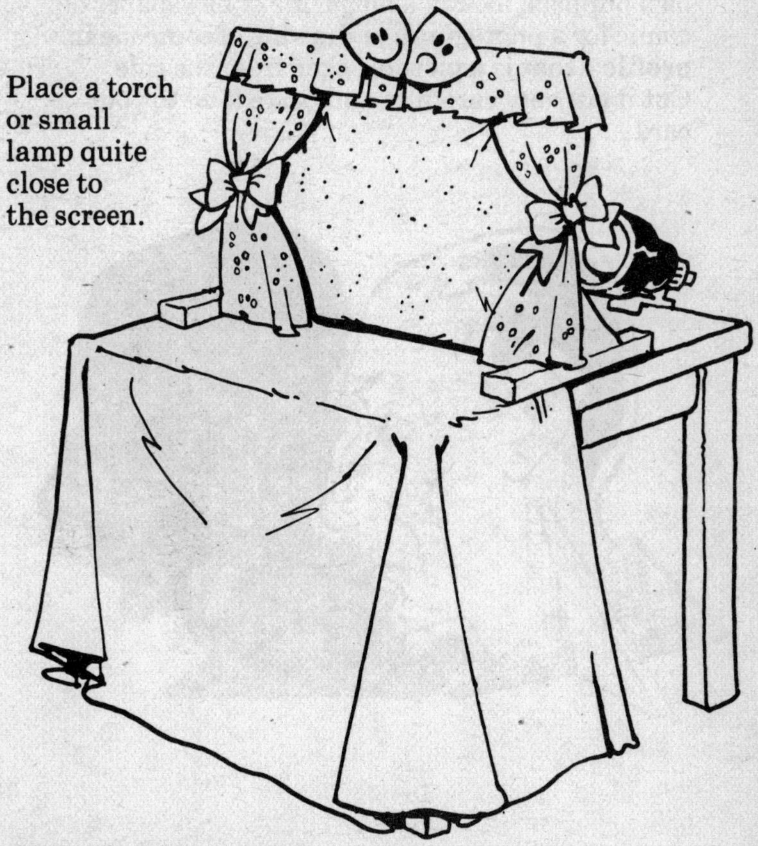

Do remember to place a cloth over the table so that your audience cannot see you hiding underneath it!

All you need now are some shadow puppets! There are many different sorts of shadow puppet that you can make, all are quite simple and can easily be made out of card – an empty cornflake packet would be ideal.

Until you feel confident enough to design your own puppets, look in a magazine or newspaper or comic for a photograph or drawing of someone **in profile** – that is a picture taken from the side. Cut it out very carefully and paste it on to your card.

When it is dry, cut it out and you will find that you have the makings of a very good puppet – just put it up against your screen with a light behind it and look at the shadow it makes.

If you glue a **long piece of cardboard** on the back of your puppet, or better still sellotape **a thin rod or piece of dowelling** on the back this will give you a handle to hold.

Now, kneel down behind your screen put your puppets between the screen and your lamp and you can start by letting them have a boxing match!

What is a red-haired boxer's favourite drink?

Ginger punch!

Once you have the knack, try drawing a few outlines of characters for yourself. It's best to try first of all on a rough piece of paper and when you are happy with your design, copy it onto card and cut it out.

Do remember to have profiles (side views) only, and keep your puppets in proportion to each other – don't have a fifteen centimetre tall man and his dog thirty centimetres tall!!

Try making animals as well as people.

With a bit of care you can create your own **Punch & Judy show** complete with dog.

Now comes the next stage – **making puppets that actually move**!

This is a little more difficult, so don't be too ambitious to begin with. First of all you must decide upon your character and what parts are going to move.

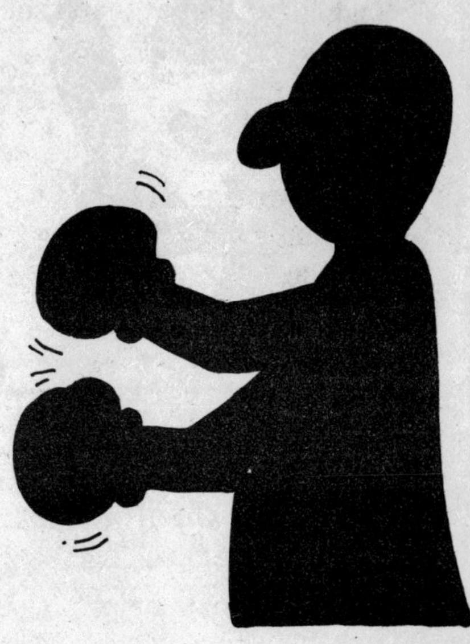

Then draw it onto cardboard and cut it out:

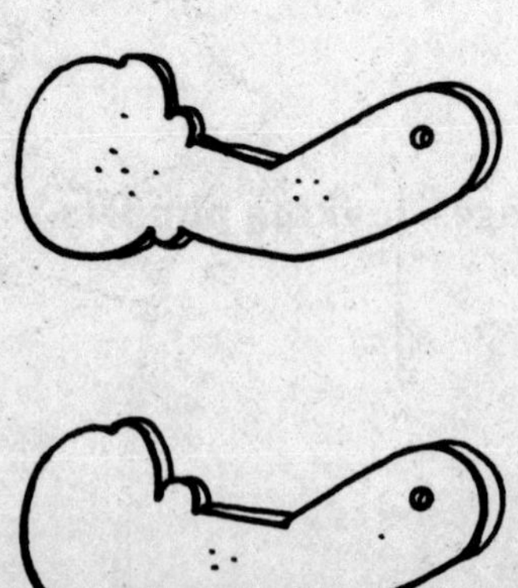

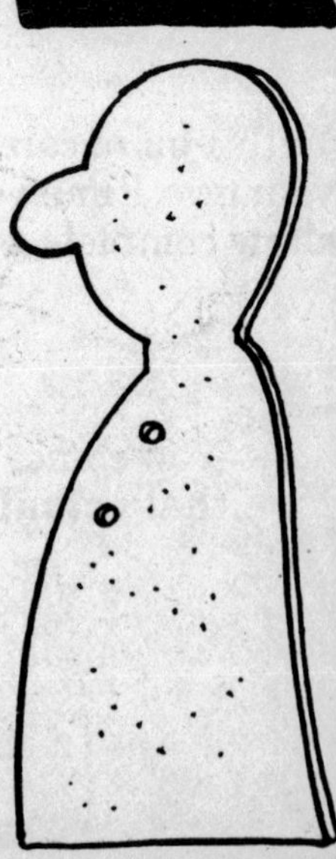

Make a small hole very carefully in each piece, get someone to help you do this. Use a spread apart metal fastener to join your puppet together, or put a piece of string through and knot it so that the joint is loose and moves very freely.

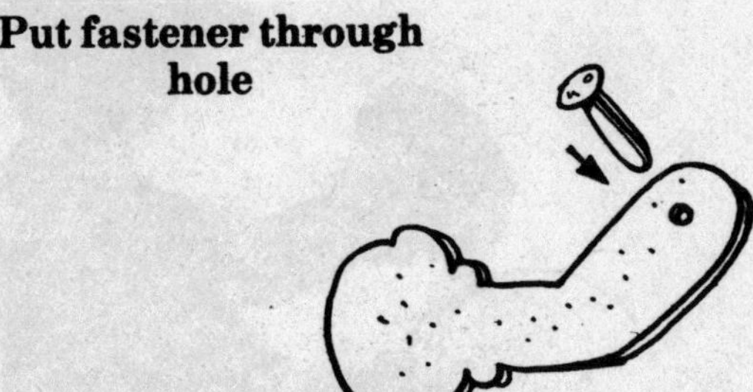

Reverse side

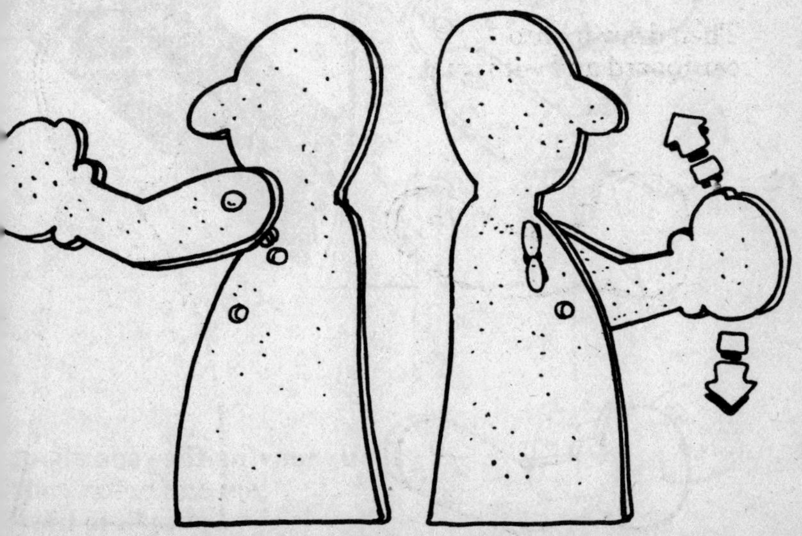

To make your shadow puppet move you need some very thin rods, preferably some stiff wire. An old knitting needle would be fine, but do **put a cork over the point** so that you don't hurt yourself.

Now attach the rods with sellotape to the moving parts.

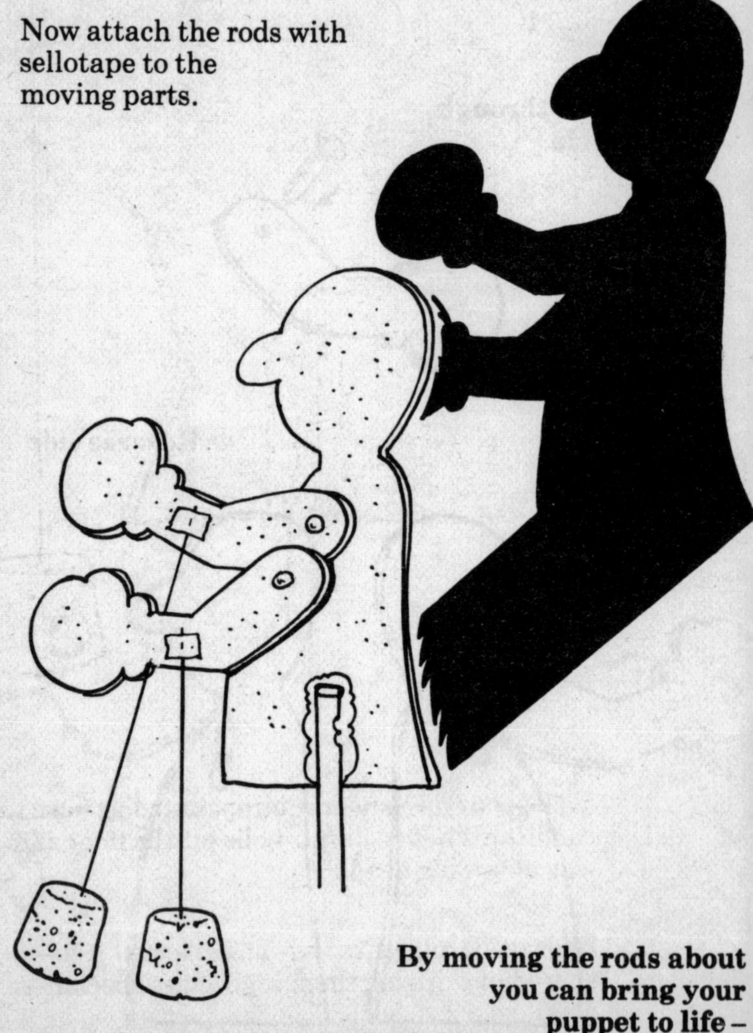

By moving the rods about you can bring your puppet to life –

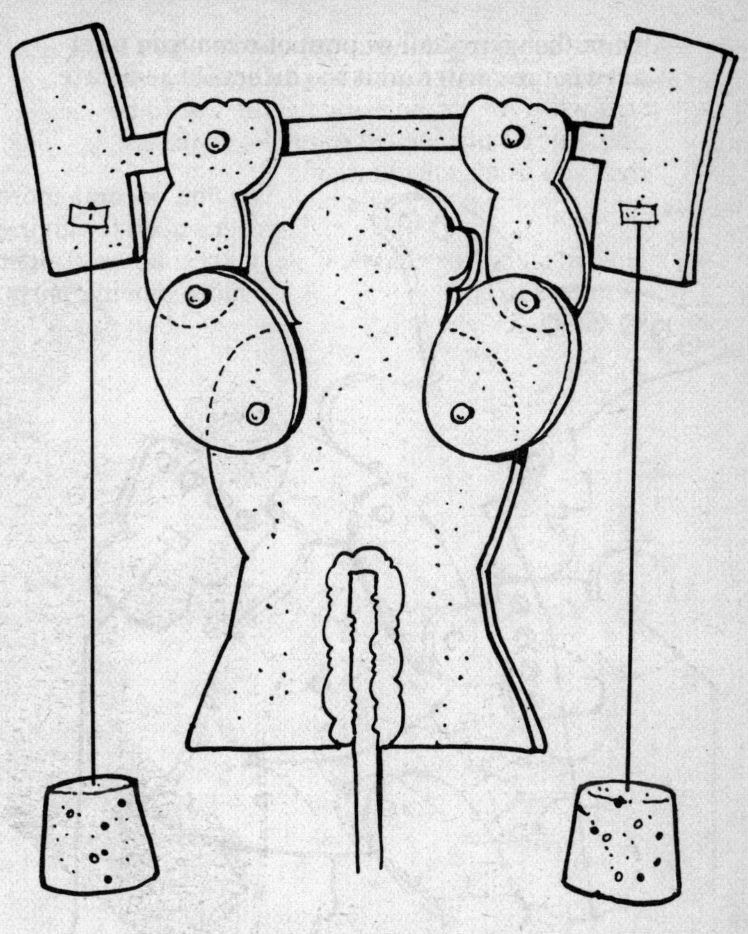

Make your own shadow puppet **strong man** who can lift his heavy dumb-bells off the floor and way above his head.

Show your audience that no expense has been spared in bringing them high-class speciality acts!

At first just give your puppet **one moving part** otherwise you will find it too difficult to operate.

As you become more experienced try giving your shadow puppet more moving parts.

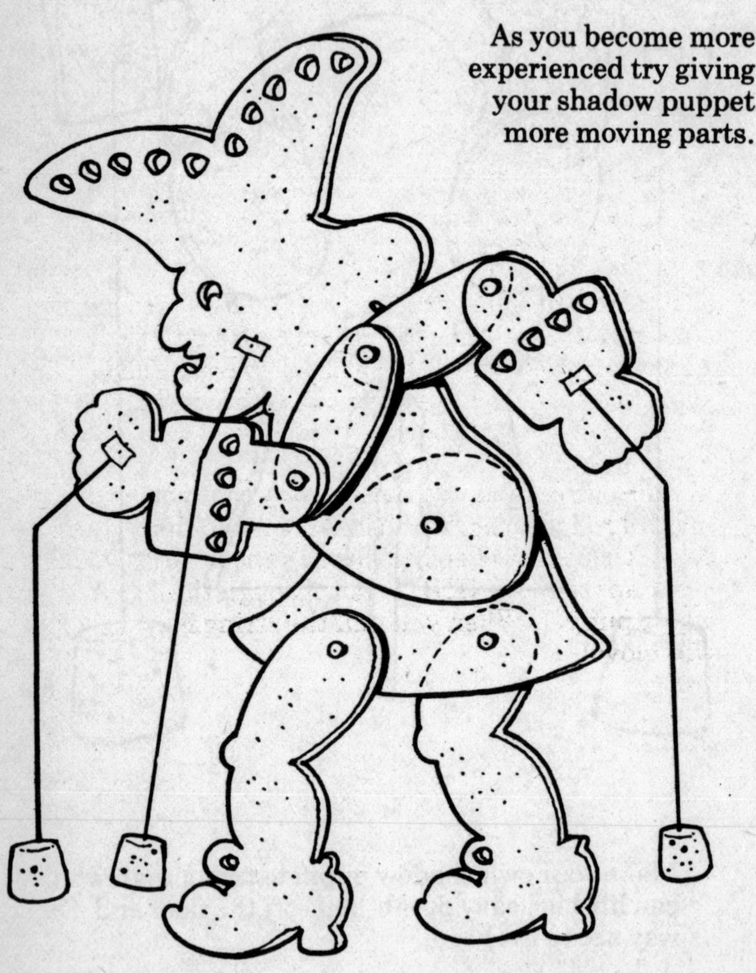

Eventually you may one day produce something like this!

Be very careful when you are cutting out the figure because the straighter your edges are then the sharper your shadow will be.

If you have no wire with which to make a rod shadow puppet – then try making a **STRING shadow puppet**, these are easy to operate and some very interesting effects can be achieved.

Make your puppet in the same way that you make a rod puppet, but instead of attaching a rod, tie a piece of string through the limb you want to move **ONLY**, not through the whole puppet. When you pull the string it will move!

If you can understand how string control puppets work then you will soon be able to make puppets of your own. Start by copying the drawing – you will see that the man is in **two pieces**, the part that moves is the separate piece – **the arm**. In the arm make two holes – one to attach it to the body, and one to put the piece of string through.

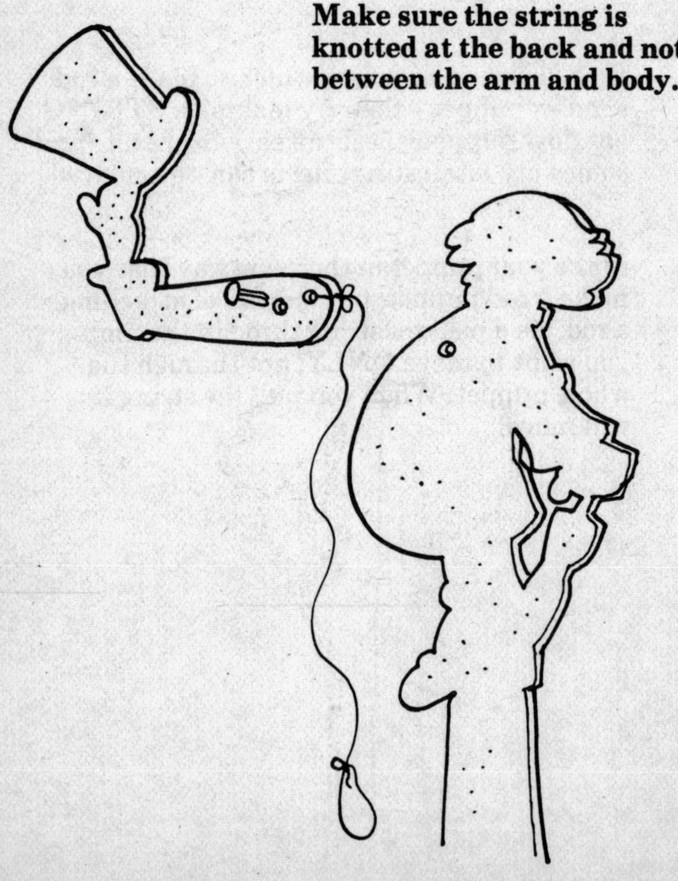

Make sure the string is knotted at the back and not between the arm and body.

All you have to do is pull the string and the man will put his hat on his head!

Now all you have to do is pull a few strings and you have a whole world of entertaining animals and people at your feet!

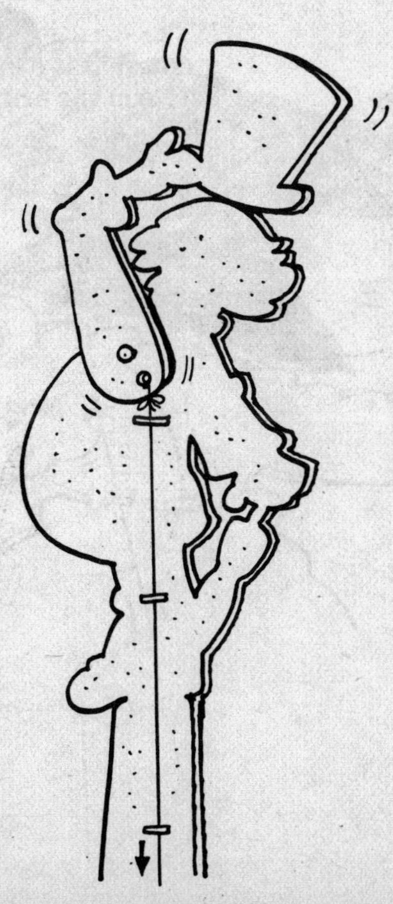

Here are a few ideas for you to copy –

A cunning crocodile

Here's an **exercising elephant**; part of your very own shadow circus. This puppet requires a great deal of concentration because there are three separate moving pieces, **the trunk, the tail** and **front leg**.

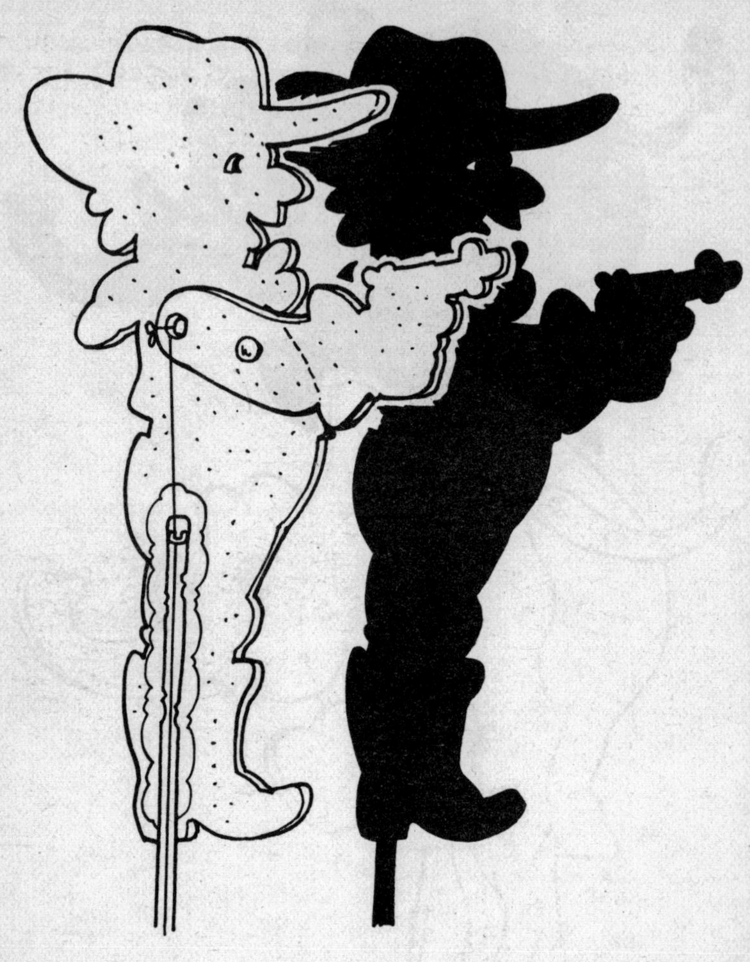

Wild Bill Hiccup, the fastest draw in the West, with a few well-chosen sound effects you can produce your own cowboy hero!

Have your very own **horse race** – or instead of a jockey, put a cowboy on the horse and include it in your western.

Bruno the Bear is always a favourite – he can open his mouth, and with just a gentle pull he can stand on his hind legs. With the help of a few friends you could perform **Goldilocks and the Three Bears** using this basic bear shape.

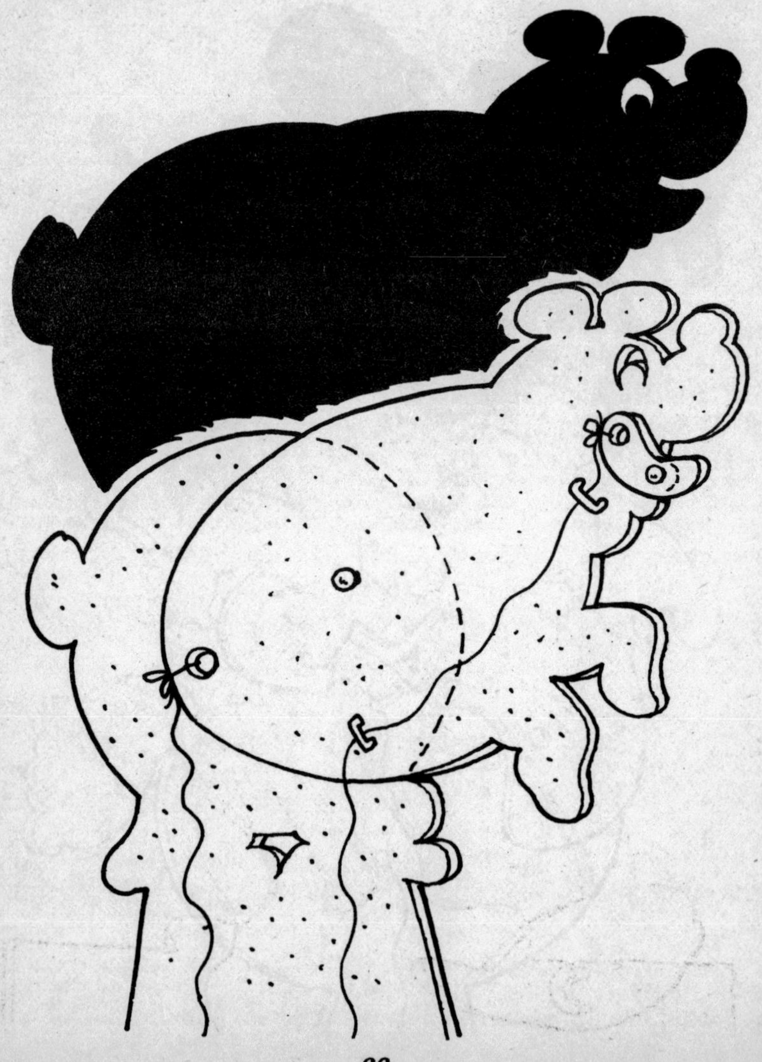

We all know how shy ostriches are, well here we have **Oswald Ostrich** who is terribly shy indeed. Just loosen the string and he'll put his head in the sand.

Just as with large-scale figure shadows, in your puppet shadow screen you can use scenery. Cut out silhouettes of trees, houses, boats, and so on, and put them right up against the screen.

Always remember to put your shadow puppets as close to the screen as you can as this will give a much clearer shadow.

If you are going to have a small puppet theatre then a **cardboard box** would be ideal – cut out a large hole in one end and put a large piece of **tracing paper** over it as a screen, and by putting your torch in the back you will have a miniature theatre – rather like a shadow television!

Finally, here is a super shadow puppet that combines both strings and rods:

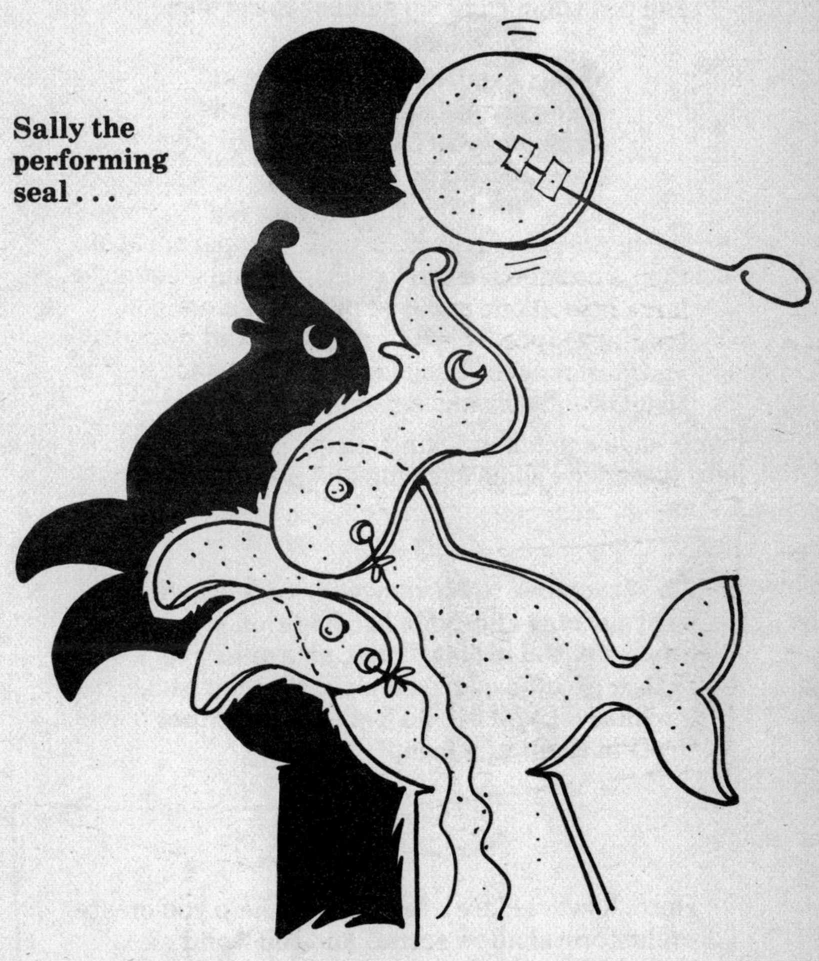

Sally the performing seal . . .

By moving the rod up and down you can bounce the ball around and let Sally catch it on her nose. A good act to finish your puppet show with.

PET SHADOWS

If you have a pet of any kind, then why not let it help you create some exciting and new shadows?

Do remember to be very very careful with your animal and *NEVER* frighten it in any way. If Tiddles Tom Cat would rather go off and catch mice then let him – whatever you do, do not force your pet to sit in front of a lamp!

Here, however, are a few ideas to help you create prehistoric shadow scenes and the world of incredible monsters!

A shadow of tiny Terry Tortoise can be turned into that of a **giant turtle** or that of a large 100 year old tortoise.

Watch him munch his way through giant sized lettuces too!

Frighten all your friends with the shadow of a long poisonous and highly dangerous **snake** –

All you need to do is dangle a worm in front of your lamp and you'll soon have the shadow of the longest and most dangerous looking python in the world.

DO NOT USE A REAL WORM!

You can fool your audience by telling them you are using a real worm (or, better still, a real rattle-snake) when in fact a **thick piece of string or cord** wiggled in a snake-like way is all you need.

Just when your sister is about to have her bath, scare her with a shadow of a terrible, ferocious **shark**.

Just when you thought it was safe to enter the water again – Jaws appears!

Place your goldfish bowl near to your lamp and see the result!

Turn even a lovable, friendly dog into the most ferocious beast imaginable! Is it **a wolf**? Or maybe it's the **Hound of the Baskervilles**!

Sit Fido in front of your lamp and see the shadow of a terrifying beast appear on your wall. Give him a bone and it will look as if this wild creature is gnawing a human limb! Or give him an old leather glove to chew and it will look as if he's bitten off someone's hand!

Is that huge shadow a lynx or a panther?

Or is it a leopard or a jaguar?

No, it's Tiddles the cat who happens to be resting in front of your lamp!

This could turn out to be a cat-astrophe! Make even your smallest kitten look like an escaped animal from the zoo and scare all your friends.

A giant **bird of prey** can easily be produced by shining a light through the budgie's cage. The resulting shadow will look like a golden eagle waiting for his lunch – or a huge black raven.

This will be the first eagle ever to shout

"Who's a pretty boy!"

Here we have a shadow of a horrible **space monster** – look at its two huge antennae – or could it be some greedy gigantic slug?

Actually it's just a common or garden **snail**! Place a torch close – or at an angle – and produce this monster from outer space!

Recreate the world of *Watership Down* with the help of your pet **rabbit**, and create your own cartoon character.

Make Bugs Bunny come alive, and feed him the largest carrot you've ever seen!

Your pet **mouse** can appear almost as large as an elephant with a little shadow trickery – now you really will have to look out for very large holes in your skirting board!

The most unusual and exciting shadows, grotesque monsters and unknown creatures from outer space, can be created from the most commonplace hamster or dog.

But do be very careful with your pet, don't upset it – especially if you happen to have a pet crocodile – otherwise it might not only be the shadow that looks dangerous!

SHADOW PLAYS

The next time you are having a party get a few friends to help you put on a complete shadow play. Often if you are playing hectic games at a party it is nice for your guests to be able to sit down and be entertained by someone else.

Alternatively you could present your very own Shadow Show. Make some tickets and invite your friends and relations round to see this unusual and much neglected form of entertainment.

Do plan your programme very carefully. Too much of one thing, however clever it may be, soon becomes dull. So present a few of your best hand shadows first of all, then perhaps a few of the shadow illusions that appear later in this book, and end with your very own **SHADOW PLAY**.

A shadow play will certainly need some preparation. So do think very carefully what you are going to do, and keep it simple.

First of all, you need a play. Very few shadow shows have actually been written, but if you have a favourite story, it can easily be turned into a shadow play. Write a script in the same way as the shadow plays given at the end of this section. Any folk story or fairy tale is ideal, and if you don't feel able to turn it into a play then simply choose one person with a good, clear and loud voice to read it aloud while you and your friends act out the movements in shadow figures.

It is important that you plan what characters you are going to use and what shadow they are going to make. Your choice of characters will often depend upon what clothes are available. Look in the section of **FIGURE SHADOWS** to get some ideas.

Once you have chosen your play, then **get together with some friends and decide who is going to play which part** – depending upon their size and shape. Someone in the group must be the **director** – he is the one who will decide how people will move, but it is best if everyone makes suggestions.

Read through the play together a few times before you start to decide on the movements.

When you do begin to work out the movements, it is best to **try them against a wall** so that you get used to working against the screen.

Remember that in a shadow play the movements are very important, and as facial expressions cannot be seen, feelings such as joy, anger, hate, sadness, or surprise have to be shown by movements of the body, arms and legs. So imagine how your character is feeling.

Here are a few movements for you to copy –

Sadness

Shock or **Horror**

You will find that the shadow play will soon begin to take shape once you have decided on a few basic moves. You will learn from mistakes and soon find which postures look the best.

After you have plotted a few basic moves, **work out what costumes you need** – the **shape is very important** and do **pay special attention to the head-dress**, as a well chosen hat will let people know immediately what you are meant to be.

Decide at this point if any scenery or props are necessary, but remember your shadow show will be much more effective if you keep it as simple as possible.

Setting up a shadow play is the same as planning a real stage play in the theatre, great attention must be paid to how it will look. Make sure that the actors stand as close to the screen as possible to get a really clear shadow.

When you feel that your play is ready for performance, **try acting the play behind your screen as you would in front of an audience.**

Set up your stage, as described earlier, and **whoever is directing should sit out front** so that he can see exactly what the audience will see and so make any necessary changes.

By kind permission of Transworld Publishers, Carousel Books now proudly present a selection of original Shadow Plays for you to perform. (And once you've tried all of these, have a go at writing your own.)

HARD TIMES By Gyles Brandreth

A shadow play in one act.

Dramatis Personae (the characters in the play)
A tramp
A man in a bowler hat (any hat will do!)
A lady
A second tramp
A pantomime horse **or** A third tramp

(Enter first tramp, walking slowly along as he speaks.)

TRAMP: Hrumph! Ohh, Hrumph! I'm so hungry . . . I haven't eaten for a week, so I'm really fed up! *(Turns around and looks)* But who's this? He looks as if he might give me the price of a chip!

(Enter a fat man in a bowler hat.)

MAN: I say! You! Have you got the time?

TRAMP: Why? What do you want?

MAN *(Shaking head)*: No, you fool, I mean, do you know what time it is?

TRAMP: No, what time is it?

MAN *(Jumping up and down in rage)*: Grrr! I don't know! I'm asking you what time it is!!

TRAMP *(Putting hand to chin in deep thought)*: I think it's . . . it's time you got a watch! *(Laughs loudly)* Ha! Ha! Good joke that – "Time you got a watch!" . . .

(Man takes cushion from under jersey, hits the tramp with it, puts it back up his jersey and goes off.)

TRAMP *(Holding head)*: Ohhh! Now I'm hungry and I've got a headache as well. Here's someone else. I hope she doesn't hit me. Perhaps she's got the price of a baked bean and an asprin!

(Enter lady with large flowery hat.)

TRAMP *(Going forward)*: Hello lady.

LADY *(Moving back quickly)*: What is it?

TRAMP: I haven't eaten all week . . .

LADY *(Shaking finger at him)*: Well, you must force yourself. It's very naughty not to eat.

(Lady goes off.)

(Another tramp comes along.)

2nd TRAMP: Hello Bill.

1st TRAMP: Hello Will – what have you got there?

2nd TRAMP: It's a cake.

1st TRAMP: I'm starving – give me half.

2nd TRAMP: No, I haven't eaten for a week. I need it all.

1st TRAMP: I haven't eaten for a week either.

2nd TRAMP: Well, you must force yourself!

1st TRAMP: Yes, I will . . . When I get my hands on that cake!

(The two go into a big tussle. They pull bits off each other. These can be bits of cloth tucked up sleeves, in collars, and into trouser tops. They poke each other in the eye, but try not to do this too realistically! They pull out bits of each other's hair – this can really be cotton wool. After a while they hit each other at the same time, and both fall down, and lie without moving. The pantomime horse, or another tramp, comes on and looks around.)

PANTOMIME HORSE: Oh, goody! A cake! It's funny that they didn't want it. Yum Yum!

(Horse makes chewing noises and goes towards the light or torch and switches it off. Everyone else gets in front of the screen, the horse-person switches on the light, lets everyone take a bow, which should be done side-on because of the shadow, and then turns off the light.)

THE END

Here's a poem for you to act – all you need are **a narrator** (someone to read aloud the poem), **a king** and **two doctors**. The king can also play the part of the **beggar**, but if you have lots of people then they can all take part, doctors by the score, couriers, 'men who would fain be rich, and rich who thought they were poor' – you can have a lot of fun miming to this . . .

THE ENCHANTED SHIRT

By Colonel John Hay

The king was sick. His cheek was red,
And his eye was clear and bright;
He ate and drank with a kingly zest,
And peacefully snored at night.

But he said he was sick – and a king should
  know;
And the doctors came by the score;
They did not cure him. He cut off their heads,
And sent to the schools for more.

At last two famous doctors came,
And one was as poor as a rat;
He had passed his life in studious toil,
And never found time to grow fat.

The other had never looked in a book;
His patients gave him no trouble:
If they recovered, they paid him well;
If they died, their heirs paid double.

Together they looked at the royal tongue,
As the king on his couch reclined;
In succession they thumped his august chest,
But no trace of disease could they find.

The old sage said, *"You're as sound as a nut!"*
"Hang him up!" roared the king in a gale –
In a ten-knot gale of royal rage;
The other leech grew a shade pale;

But he pensively rubbed his sagacious nose,
And thus his prescription ran:
"The king will be well if he sleeps one night in the shirt of a happy man."

Wide o'er the realm the couriers rode and fast their horses ran,
And many they saw, and to many they spake,
But they found no happy man.

They found poor men who would fain be rich,
And rich who thought they were poor;
And men who twisted their waists in stays,
And women that short hose wore.

They saw two men by the roadside sit,
And both bemoaned their lot;
For one had buried his wife, he said,
And the other one had not.

At last they came to a village gate;
A beggar lay whistling there;
He whistled and sang and laughed and rolled
On the grass in the soft June air.

The weary couriers paused and looked
At the scamp so blithe and gay,
And one of them said, *"Heaven save you, friend,
You seem to be happy today."*

"Oh yes, fair sirs," the rascal laughed,
And his voice rang free and glad;
*"An idle man has so much to do
That he never has time to be sad."*

"This is our man," the courier said;
*"Our luck has led us aright.
I will give you a hundred ducats, friend,
For the loan of your shirt tonight."*

The merry blackguard lay back on the grass,
And laughed till his face was black;
"I would do it, God wot," and he roared with fun,
"But I haven't a shirt to my back!"

THE END

Try acting out a favourite poem of yours, but find one that has some recognisable characters, like a king, and one that also tells a little story too.

At Christmas why not present your very own shadow pantomime –

SHADOWELLA

Dramatis Personae

Shadowella
Buttons/Narrator
Fatface } Ugly Sisters
Bignose }
Fairy Godmother
Prince Charming

NARRATOR: Long long ago there was a beautiful girl who lived with her two very ugly sisters. Her two sisters always liked to be in the limelight and so pushed her into the shadows – which is how she came to be called Shadowella. But Shadowella was very sad . . .

(Enter SHADOWELLA – *head down, looking sad.)*

SHADOWELLA: Oh Buttons, I'm so very sad . . . my sisters are so nasty to me they are wearing me to a shadow.

BUTTONS: Why, what have they done?

SHADOWELLA: Well, they make me do all the washing, the ironing, the cooking. I never get time to eat. Now we have received invitations to a huge ball that Prince Charming is holding and they have torn up my invitation.

BUTTONS: Oh dear, Shadowella – please don't cry, I think you're wonderful, even if they don't.

SHADOWELLA: Oh Buttons, you're so kind.

BUTTONS: Yes, I am aren't I. I was wondering if . . . er, . . . well, if you would give me a little kiss on the cheek?

SHADOWELLA: Yes, of course Buttons, but close your eyes.

BUTTONS: O.K.

SHADOWELLA: Are they shut really tight?

BUTTONS: Yes, very tight.

(Enter FATFACE *and* BIGNOSE *– they push* SHADOWELLA *off stage, and stand each side of* BUTTONS *ready to kiss him.)*

BUTTONS: Come on Shadowella, hurry up.

(Turns his head from side to side – sees the Ugly Sisters – screams and runs off stage.)

FATFACE: Funny man, it must have been your ugly face that scared him off.

BIGNOSE: How dare you – you're only jealous of my beautiful figure.

FATFACE: Jealous! It's like an overweight jersey.

BIGNOSE: Pullover?

FATFACE: No, cow!

*(*FATFACE *hits* BIGNOSE *with her handbag.)*

BIGNOSE: Come on, it's time for our Keep Fit Class on the radio, I'll turn it on.

(Fetches a cardboard box that gives a radio shadow.)

VOICE: This is the BBC. Welcome to "Keep Fit", this is Miss. Bendown. Now girls, here is a good exercise for your legs. Stand up straight and grasp something solid.

(They grasp each other.)

Now lift your left leg, put it behind you and hold it with your hand.

(They lift their legs and fall on top of each other.)

FATFACE *(Gasping)*: I need a drink of milk after that.

(They both exit. Enter BUTTONS.*)*

BUTTONS: While they've gone I'll change the station – they'll never notice.

(Picks up radio and mimes turning a knob. Exit BUTTONS.*)*

VOICE: This is Fanny Haddock in the kitchen, telling you how to prepare steak for the oven.

(Enter FATFACE *and* BIGNOSE.*)*

FATFACE: Let's carry on with our exercises.

VOICE: Now, put your rump on a nice cool surface.

(They both sit down.)

And hit it hard to make it tender.

(They turn and look at each other.)

Then place it in some gravy.

BIGNOSE: I'm turning this off. It's the last time I do any exercises. Let's get ready for the ball.

FATFACE: Yes, I'm going to wear my Bargain Frock.

BIGNOSE: Oh, you mean the one you got for that ridiculous figure!

FATFACE: Shadowella!

(Enter SHADOWELLA.*)*

FATFACE: Shadowella! While we're away clean this house from top to bottom. Now, call me a carriage.

(Exit UGLY SISTERS.*)*

SHADOWELLA: You old carriage!

SHADOWELLA: Oh dear – I'm so sad. I wish I could go to the ball.

(Enter FAIRY GODMOTHER.*)*

FAIRY GODMOTHER: Don't be sad – you shall go to the ball. Here's a beautiful gown.

(Throws a cloak over SHADOWELLA, *which will give the shadow of a long gown.)*

SHADOWELLA: *Oh, it's beautiful!*

FAIRY GODMOTHER: Now fetch me a pumpkin.

*(*SHADOWELLA *gives her a cardboard cut-out of a pumpkin – the* FAIRY GODMOTHER *waves her arms and it turns into a carriage – all you need are a cardboard pumpkin and a cardboard carriage. As the* FAIRY GODMOTHER *waves her arms the pumpkin can be laid flat so that it will disappear – and if the carriage is placed close to the lamp it will give the*

shadow of a huge carriage. It will take a little practice – but try it and see.)

You may find it easier for someone to quickly turn off the lamp and put the carriage in place as the Godmother waves her arms – making it look like a flash.

FAIRY GODMOTHER: Now hurry to the ball, but be sure to leave by midnight or your gown will turn to rags.

(Now get someone to turn the light off for a couple of minutes while the cut-out of the carriage is removed. Exit SHADOWELLA *and* FAIRY GODMOTHER.*)*

(Enter BUTTONS.*)*

BUTTONS: Shadowella had a marvellous time at the ball and the Prince fell madly in love with her. But as the Fairy Godmother foretold, at the stroke of midnight her gown turned to rags and Shadowella ran all the way home, leaving behind her one glass slipper.

(Exit BUTTONS. *Enter* UGLY SISTERS.*)*

BIGNOSE: I was the most beautiful at the ball last night.

FATFACE: You couldn't have been. I was there!

(Enter PRINCE CHARMING.*)*

PRINCE: You have heard my decree. Whoever this slipper fits, I will marry.

FATFACE: I'll try it, it's obviously me you should marry.

BIGNOSE: It won't fit your clodhopper, it's more like a yard than a foot. Let me try!

(They fight over the slipper.)

(Enter FAIRY GODMOTHER.*)*

FAIRY GODMOTHER: If you try the slipper on Shadowella's foot you will see that it fits.

(The PRINCE *tries the slipper on* SHADOWELLA*'s foot.)*

PRINCE: Why it fits! Shadowella, you shall be my bride!

*(*THE UGLY SISTERS *scream and run off stage one each side.* SHADOWELLA *and the* PRINCE *walk to the back of the stage, past the lamp which means the stage will be empty.)*

(Enter BUTTONS.*)*

BUTTONS: Shadowella married the prince and left her Ugly Sisters and went to live at the palace. I never did get that kiss.

(Enter UGLY SISTERS, *one from each side.)*

FATFACE & BIGNOSE: Don't worry you still have us!

(They stand in silhouette of kissing position as before.)

THE END

To add a touch of professionalism to your shadow play, **try also making a silhouette of the title of the play** by carefully cutting out the letters on a piece of cardboard:–

Make a stencil of the title of your play and shine the light through it.

If you find making a stencil difficult, write the letters on to card, and cut them out.

Sellotape a piece of cotton to each letter, or perhaps two so that it remains still and tie them to a rod. Hold it in front of your lamp and it makes a perfect ending to any shadow play!

SHADOW MAGIC

You can do many amazing and incredible tricks with shadows and create astounding illusions that you never thought possible. It's all great fun.

But make sure that you don't ever tell your friends, or the audience, the secrets of shadow magic and they'll really believe that you are a very clever magician.

Did you hear about the magician on board a ship? Every time he made something disappear a parrot would shout *"Rubbish! Rubbish!"* One day the ship sank. All that was left was a plank with the parrot and the magician sitting on it. The parrot said: *"O.K. clever, what have you done with the ship?"*

When performing shadow magic pay careful attention to how you dress – should you wear a fez like Tommy Cooper or a pointed hat and cloak and look just like a real wizard? It's all part of your **"image"**.

Begin the shadow magic act with a few quite simple illusions. **First make an enormous tree from a small plant:–**

To prepare this trick, roll some sheets of newspaper together to form a tube –

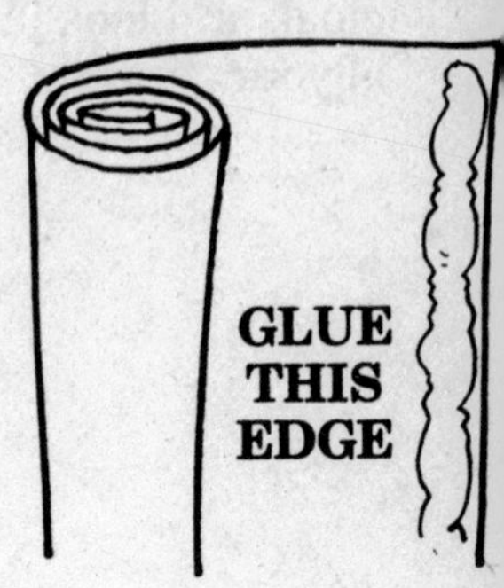

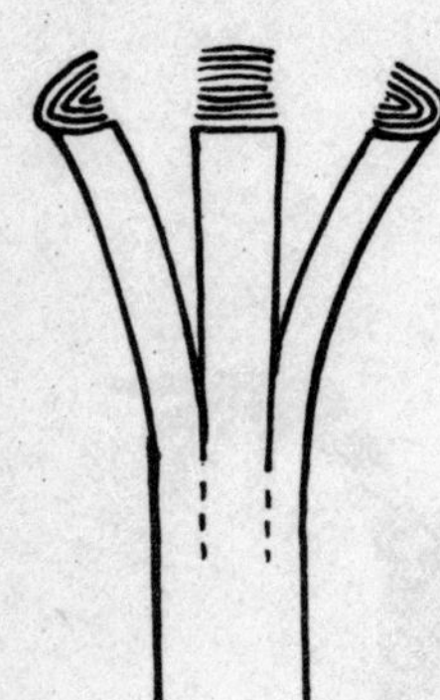

Cut down the tube about 15 centimetres –

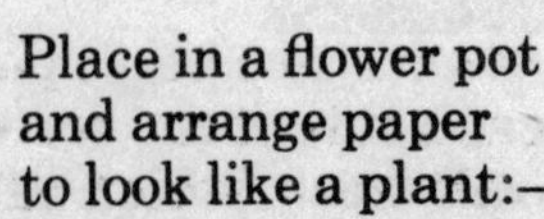

Place in a flower pot and arrange paper to look like a plant:–

When you do the trick, just pull it carefully from the top and it will magically grow. Remember, the more layers you have the taller the tree will grow.

If you open your act with two plant pots like these, one on each side of the screen, you can make two tall trees, which can stand there throughout the rest of the performance.

A **ladder** can be made in a similar way:–

Just cut out the middle section of your tube.

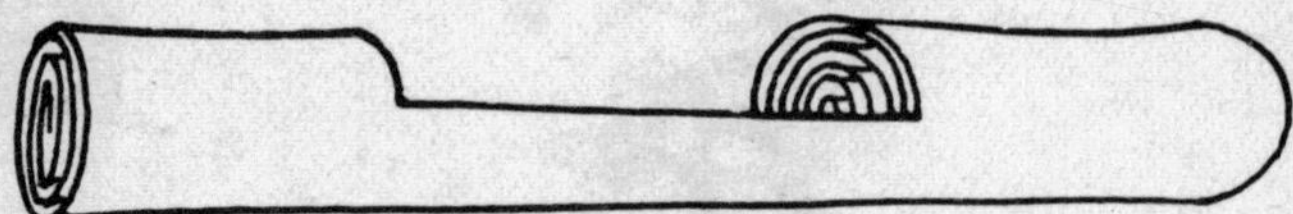

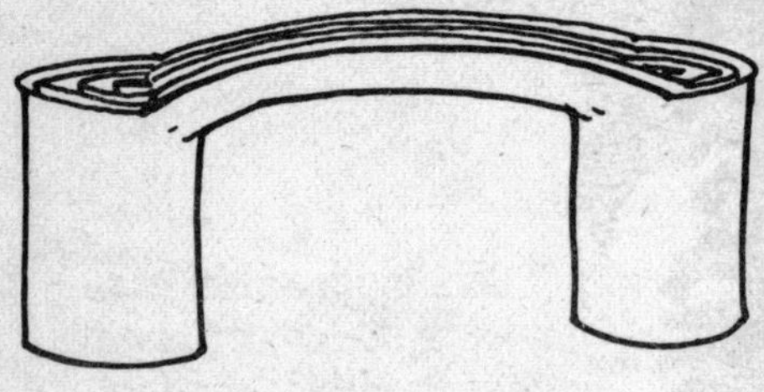

Fold it in half

and pull!

This could be your ladder to success!

Learn the art of levitation – making things mysteriously rise up in the air on their own.

Fix a very thin wire or piece of cotton to a hat or similar object. Because the light will only cast a shadow of you and the object you can make it seem to rise up into the air by itself.

Now astound everyone by producing a long line of silk scarves out of one handkerchief!

Quite simple – just show your audience one handkerchief. Screw it up in your hand and then pull from your hand a long line of handkerchiefs or silk scarves that you have already tucked up your sleeve.

Because this is a shadow magic show the audience will not see where the silks come from, they will appear to come from nowhere!

It is useful if you are able to have a little table behind the screen with you. Make sure that it has a cloth on it, and pin to the cloth a little bag for this next trick.

You will also need a hollow cardboard tube.

You show this tube to the audience in such a way that the shadow shows them it is empty. Then you stand the tube on the table and miraculously you begin to pull all sorts of objects out of it, even though you can at any time display that the tube is empty.

What you in fact do is have your objects hidden in the bag pinned to the cloth – keep the tube close to the edge of the table so that you can reach through the tube and into the bag.

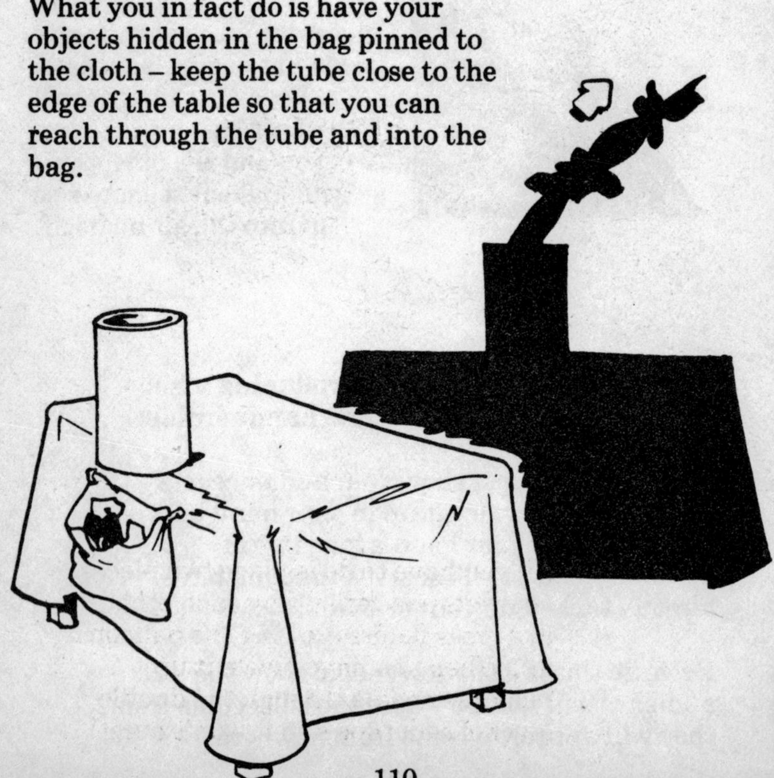

At the end you can take the cloth off to show there are no holes in it and that nobody is hidden under the table!

Astound your audience by blowing up a balloon and then push a large knitting needle into it without bursting it.

All you have to do is place two pieces of sellotape overlapping each other in a cross before blowing the balloon up. When you have blown it up, push the needle through the double layer of sellotape and it won't burst!

Other great illusions can also be achieved with shadow magic. Get an assistant to help you with these tricks, but only he must know the secrets.

Ask him to hand you an iron bar, and then show your amazing strength by bending it.

All you need is a tightly rolled up newspaper – the shadow will make it look like a rod of iron.

Make your assistant stand in the centre of the stage, cover him with a sheet, and then stick sharp and dangerous swords through him!

This can be achieved by having swords made out of cardboard and pushing them under his arms. If he holds his arms tightly by his sides you will be able to tuck two or three under each arm.

Slowly pull them out again, and lo and behold! Your assistant is unharmed!

Have a magical fight with your partner to the amusement of your audience . . .

Instead of facing each other, stand a little to one side of each other – the shadow will make it look as if you are exactly opposite each other.

Now you can have a boxing match – just punch in front of you, the shadows will look as if they are actually hitting each other!

Throw a bucket of water over your friend! All you need is a bucket full of little torn scraps of paper, the shadow will look like water!

Finally, pull pieces off each other! You should have pieces of cotton wool and cloth hidden up your sleeves and down your collars – when you pull them out the shadow will look frightening, but it really is all an illusion!

And now . . . the greatest illusion of all time . . . the tight-rope walker!

You will need **a plank of wood** supported by **two chairs**. Get some friends off stage to hold the ends of the plank to make it firm. If you rest the plank on two chairs the shadow will look like a thin string. Dressed in a ballet skirt or swimming costume walk along the plank, putting one foot carefully in front of the other. It really will give the illusion of a tight-rope walker!

Always choose the order of your acts very carefully. Start with something quite simple and work up to a big spectacular illusion to end with. One of the best ways to end your act is to make yourself disappear altogether! (See below!)

It helps if you can **have some music playing quietly** while you are performing and do **be sure to position yourself to one side** so that the audience can see exactly what you are doing.

Here is one of the greatest illusions of all time! Your audience will be breathless as you jump into the air and totally vanish!

Here is the big, big secret – don't tell anyone how it's done . . .

When you have finished your shadow show just walk back towards your lamp – this will make your shadow increase in size, and then simply jump over your lamp – once you are behind it there will be no shadow. To the audience it will seem as if you jumped into the air and vanished!

It's pure magic!

SHADOW GAMES

Making shadows can be as much fun as playing a game, so at your next party why not include a few shadow games for your friends. In your great-grandfather's time shadow games were a very popular amusement, but today they would seem new and certainly a novelty at any party. Even grown-ups can take part.

Some of the shadow games will need a little preparation beforehand, and it might be a nice idea to give a small prize or two – perhaps have a big bag of sweets so that eventually everyone will get a prize!

Here are some games that can be played with any amount of people –

Shadow Buff

This is a popular Victorian version of Blind Man's Buff. For this you will need **a large sheet** and **a lamp**, as with the figure shadows, and **a few props** – such as hats and scarves.

Choose one person to be the "Guesser", and everyone else goes behind the screen, he stays in front of it. One of the people behind the screen casts a shadow on the screen and the "Guesser" has to call out the person's name – he is allowed three guesses. If he guesses correctly then he joins the others behind the screen and the one casting the shadow becomes the guesser.

It is important that the person casting the shadow disguises himself to fool the guesser by screwing up his face, ruffling up his hair, putting on a false nose, or a hat. This game can bring hours of hilarious fun.

Shadow Charades

Another Victorian game – this time divide everyone into **two teams**.

Each team must then be given some pieces of paper on which you have written the title of **a nursery rhyme, a book**, or **television programme**. Then get two or three from each team to go behind the screen and mime what is written on the paper.

The other team must guess what is being mimed.

Here are a few suggestions:–

MARY HAD A LITTLE LAMB
HUMPTY DUMPTY
HEY DIDDLE DIDDLE
JACK AND JILL
POLLY PUT THE KETTLE ON
DING DONG BELL
SING A SONG OF SIXPENCE

Guess What?

Here is a game that you will need to get ready beforehand. Gather together **a few everyday objects**, from saucepans to hairbrushes, and **a few unusual ones,** too.

You will need a small table behind your screen. Lay each object down one at a time on the table – everyone else must guess what the object is.

To make things especially hard, place your lamp to one side or at an unusual angle so that it casts an interesting shadow without giving too much away!

Guess Who?

This is a similar game to "Guess What?" but this time try and find some **photographs in profile of your favourite TV stars or cartoon characters**, try drawing or copying them if you are really clever. Stick them on to thin card and cut them out so that you have a silhouette of each person. This time, however, put your cut-out as close to the screen as possible to get a really clear shadow.

They'll feel a right Charlie if they don't get this one –

that silent screen favourite, **Charlie Chaplin**!

Snoopy

This shadow might just fox them! But I doubt it – it's that lovable friendly fox, **Basil Brush**.

You will need a good **eye** to **sea** this one!

Yes, it's that lovable spinach eating sailor – **Popeye.**

Just for fun – include this in your shadow game – of course, there is nothing there at all! But tell your friends that it is the shadow of a person and they'll all look very carefully thinking that their eyes are deceiving them. When they give up tell them it is a shadow of the **Invisible Man**!

A very royal shadow this one – it would be nice to end your "Guess Who?" game with a profile of this gracious lady –

Her Majesty the Queen.

Find a friend

This game will cause a lot of fun and will also give your guests a permanent souvenir of your party to take home with them.

It will take a little time, so it is best to prepare this in another room while your guests are enjoying themselves playing another game elsewhere.

What you need is your shadow screen and some large pieces of paper. Invite your guests in one at a time and get them to sit behind the screen and cast a shadow.

If you stand on the other side of the screen and hold up a large sheet of paper, you should easily be able to trace the outline of your friend's face onto the paper.

When you have finished them, pin them up around the room and then invite everyone in to guess who each silhouette belongs to, and if you have been very careful they should be instantly recognisable.

At the end of the party let each friend take home his or her shadow portrait – if they are cut out and mounted onto black card, they will make delightful presents for grandmas and aunts!

By now you will be a shadow expert, without a shadow of a doubt! If you take a lot of care and practice, you will soon be producing some very professional shadow shows. People will enjoy watching your shadows but also being able to actively take part in the games you play. Everyone will want to come to your parties!

Your own shadow has been with you all your life, make friends with him now – he's your inseparable companion and follows you everywhere. Just watch him and he will take you and introduce you into the shadow world – a world where anything can happen!

The key to the Shadow World
is at your finger tips!!

We are no other than a moving row
Of magic shadow shapes that
come and go
Round with the sun-illumin'd lantern
held
In midnight by the Master of the
show.

The Rubaiyat of Omar Khayyam